MAN IN KĀVYA

Usharbudh Arya

MOTILAL BANARSIDASS
DELHI :: VARANASI :: PATNA

Head Office BUNGALOW ROAD, JAWAHARNAGAR, DELHI-7
Branch Offices : (i) CHOWK, VARANASI (U.P.)
(ii) ASHOK RAJ PATH, PATNA (BIHAR)

FIRST EDITION
1971

Printed in India
BY SHANTILAL JAIN AT SHRI JAINENDRA PRESS, BUNGALOW ROAD, JAWAHARNAGAR, DELHI-7, AND PUBLISHED BY SUNDAR LAL JAIN FOR MOTILAL BANARSIDASS, BUNGALOW ROAD, JAWAHARNAGAR, DELHI 7.

MAN IN KAVYA

Diverse statements can be made concerning the place the Indian mind assigns to man in the nature of things. On one hand there is the inward reflectiveness and preoccupation with universals[1] which might preclude any involvement with emotions, problems and stresses of practical life, based on negating external realities and following Vedantic idealism, emphasizing withdrawal, *nivṛtti*. On the other hand is the *Mīmāṁsā* emphasis on action[2] and the presence of well known texts on practical life and prudence, *nīti*, as well as practical sciences. In a third category is the reconciliation of the two views. The *Bhagavadgītā* speaks of *karma-sanyāsa* or yoga and *karma-yoga* or *sāṅkhya* being complementary. *Artha* and *kāma* are included among the four purposes of man, *puruṣārthas*.

Indian literature can be divided into three sections each supporting one of the above three views, with its ownemphasis and interpretation of aspects of cosmology, metaphysics, man's nature, conduct, needs and reactions to his environment.

The poetry, drama and narrative prose literature in Sanskrit, *kāvya*, has been so far ignored in trying to ascertain the Indian view of man. It has been studied with application of literary theories laid down and discussed by the authors on poetics, *kāvya-śāstra*. The epics are regarded by these *kāvya-śāstra* authors as great works of literature, *mahākāvyas*, and by religious philosophers as scriptural texts, *dharmaśāstras*; it is difficult to assign them either one of these two places. However, the epic view of man has been studied in some detail. It is proposed in this paper to study the *kāvya* works not as to their aesthetic or literary quality but as they express certain ideas and attitudes regarding man's place in an over all scheme. The *mahākāvyas* will find only a contextual reference. The *kāvya-śāstra* works will be quoted where contributive to an understanding of the nature of man in *kāvya*. In view of an abundance of material in *kāvya* texts only selective examples will be given, mainly from *Bhāsa*, *Śūdraka*, *Kālidāsa*, and *Bhavabhūti*. Works like *Nāgānanda*, which were inspired from an exclusive ideal, are not used as they are not representative of the general *kāvya* view.

MAN'S GOALS

We present the hyposthesis that *kāvya* reflects the third position which synthesizes without denying either of the first two and thus refutes a possible exclusive view that Indian outlook is not concerned with man as an individual and with his involvement in external realities.

Kāvya deals with human characters, their exploits and experiences. Since these experiences are of worldly reality, *laukika*, is there any attempt to resolve the Hindu dichotomy between the vulgar and the scriptural, *laukika* and *vaidika*[3], the practical consideration as against textual injunction, *loka* and *śāstra*, the discussion of which often appears in works on secular sciences such as grammar and logic ? In these the *śāstra* is regarded as the regulator of what otherwise in the ordinary worldly life might become unregulated behaviour.[4] The purpose of such regulation is said to be to enhance the desired worldly success, comfort and peace—in one word, *abhyudaya*—which the *Vaiśeṣika-sūtras* (I.1) include in the purpose of *dharma* along with *summum bonum*, *niḥ-śreyasa*. Does *kāvya* subscribe to this arrangement ? Mukherji[5] lists the views of various authors on *kāvya-śāstra* from *Bharata* onwards on "benefits accruing from poetry" by which he means the purpose of *kāvya*. It is noteworthy that most of these *śāstrakāras* in one way or another accept the four *puruṣārthas* including *dharma* and otherworldly benefits as accruing from *kāvya*. This also explains the previously mentioned dual nature of the epics as works of literature as well as religious texts. Many *śāstrakāras* also include such advantages of *kāvya* creativity as fame and profit along with aesthetic fulfilment. Of all the authors *Bhoja* in his *Śṛṅgāra-prakāśa* is the most elaborate on *dharma*. In explaining various types of the poetic sentiment of love and eros, *śṛṅgāra*, he counts the love of righteousness, *dharma-śṛṅgāra*, as the first.[6]

Some of the theorists such as *Abhinavagupta* and *Jagannātha* have also exalted the aesthetic pleasure, *rasa*, by considering it as proceeding from the Vedantic *Brahman's* reservoir of bliss, *ānanda*. The theorists of poetic suggestion, *dhvani*, also hint at *ānanda* being the ultimate proceed of the pleasure derived from *kāvya*.[7] Within that context, the search for man's true character and role has never ceased. From *Bharata* to *Jagannātha* thinkers developed many theories, successively rejecting or incorporating any earlier ones in proposing and developing their systems. The number of the nuances of human emotion, *rasas*, has been debated throughout.[8] What appears to be a fixation with stylized categories is merely a broad outline within which a great variety of ideas has been proposed and examined. For example, when it was found that *sṛṅgāra* did not cover the non-erotic love and affection, the *preyān* category[9] was introduced. Without going into these theories which have been amply discussed by other authors, we may briefly assert that Sanskrit writers on aesthetics have echoed ancient texts on other sciences and regard *kāvya* to be just another means of man to fulfil himself through the four ends of man (*puruṣārthas*) namely, pursuit of virtue (*dharma*), gaining material means (*artha*), fulfilling worldly desires (*kāma*) and attaining the *summum bonum* (*mokṣa*). Thus the pursuit of life's material needs and emotions is not excluded but these must in turn be subjugated to the metaphysical scheme of *dharma*, *mokṣa* and the universals.[10]

How far can these views of the theorists be substantiated by an actual look at the *kāvya* works ? We examine this first by looking for the *kāvya* attitude to the textual world view.

REVEALED AUTHORITY

Having been composed by brahmins it is natural that *kāvya* works should reflect the Vedic erudition and conform with traditions and laws. It is not necessary to go ino details of this tradition as pervading the *kāvya*. Here and there attempts were made even to compose verses in the then archaic Vedic style. *Kālidāsa* has only rare examples of this : *Abhijñānaśākuntala* (IV.8)[11] being the best copy of the Vedic style while

IV.4, 7 are examples of verses only partially in that style. *Bhavabhūti*, proudest of his brahminhood among the playwrights, demonstrates his facility with Vedic usage more often. In his view, "words of the contemporary (*laukika*) poets follow their intent whereas with the early Vedic sages meaning follows the inspired word" *URC*[12] (I.10). Thus he even prefers to use Vedic names and epithets for his deities; e.g. *URC.* in II.3 the Vedic sages as *udgītha-vid.* The words, phrases, entire lines are borrowed or paraphrased from Vedic passages. I.15, II.12, V.10, and sentences following,[13] IV.18, V.27, 29, 30, VI.14, 22, VII.4, 17 are strongly reminscent of Vedic hymns. A Vedic epithet for fire-god (uṣarbudha) occurs after VI.4, the only place outside *Ṛgveda.* The entire *kāvya* literature is replete with references to *yajña, tapas, mantras, ṛṣis,* Vedic divine figures and such, so as to render redundant any attempt at proving that *śruti* and *smṛti* authorities are accepted beyond question.

MAN IN COSMOLOGY

Are there any clear views on cosmology ? In *Kālidāsa's* works we find echoes of the religio-philosophical literature such as *Kaṭha* and *Śvetaśvatara Upaniṣads, Bhagavadgītā* and *Manu.* There does not seem a clear distinction between theistic *Sāṅkhya* and *Vedānta*, and the passages may be quoted or interpreted to support either view. It is possible that *Sāṅkhya* and *Vedānta* are deliberately reconciled in passages such as *KS.* II.13. Some of the more important passages, explaining, supplementing and enhancing the points made in the religio-philosophical texts, are translated in the appendix. There *RV.*[14] X.22, 23-36, 29, *KS.*[15] II.7, VI. 77 especially indicate man's divine origin, the difference of sexes arising from the Primal Force dividing Itself into two, the undesirability of the worldly cycles of birth and death (*saṁsāra*), the freedom from which is gained by ascetic devotion to God without infrining the requirements of the four ends which, again, include *artha* and *kāma*

DIVINE NATURE OF MAN

The place of man in *Kāvya* may be challenged on the

grounds that many of the heroes and characters are often divine and semi-divine figures.[16] The hero of a *nāṭaka* may be a *deva*. In *samavakāra* and *īhamṛga* types of drama also the celestial figures play important roles.[17] The hero of *Kumārasambhava* is *Śiva* himself, not a human being. But the distinctions between human and divine are very vague.

The *aṁśāvatāra* theory[18] stipulates that all individual souls (*jīvas*) are part emanations descended from God and thus carry His divine nature in them. A hero may be a man among gods and a god among men, a woman of extraordinary beauty is no ordinary human, nor can a very attractive person simply be a mortal (*Avimāraka* II. 5ff., IV. 12ff.).

Because the *nāṭaka* form of drama has to serve as the prototype of, the ideal for, other forms of lesser level, such as *prakaraṇa* (*Daśarūpaka* III.1), with human heroes less endowed with divine qualities, the heroes of *nāṭakas* are not *devas* alone; the idea is to have exalted ideal figures. "A high-born sage king, divine or semidivine person should be the hero of a *nāṭaka*, a splendrous personality of steadfast and exalted, *dhīrodātta* type"[19] (*Sāhityadarpaṇa* VI. 9)[20]. Not all authors, however, agree with the rule. *Nāṭyadarpaṇa*[21] protests that since gods can attain everything by their will alone, it leaves little scope for developing conflicts in the plot. The objection can be met by pointing out that actually there is no drama in Sanskrit with a purely divine figure free of a human guise. In *KS*. *Śiva* is at least once disturbed and agitated when the first arrow of *Kāma* is shot at him (III.66-67). He is depicted in a human form and therefore not beyond participation in romance, marriage, sexual consummation and begetting a son. He is involved in the conflicts and crises that develop among the personae of the plot around him.

It is through the device of imposing humanity on the celestial and heavenliness on the human characters that a constant intercourse between human and celestial figures is created. Born of a celestial nymph, *Śakuntalā* is a human child at whose hour of woe a heavenly hand is extended (*AŚ*. VI.

29-30, VII. 1ff.). *Vikrama Purūravas* is declared to have had sun and the moon for maternal and paternal grandfathers (*VU.* IV.38). He helps the nymphs besieged by *rākṣasas* (*VU.* I.1) and marries *Urvaśī.* Gods fear men (*RV.* V.29) and men and gods battle against each other (*RV.* III. 52 ff.). Men become instruments of releasing fallen celestial beings from effects of heavenly curses (*RV.* V. 51ff.). Celestial beings shower flowers at the successes of their favorite men on earth (*RV.* II.60, IV. 19). The celestial beings are not free of mortal-like jealousies among themselves (*R.V.* VII.53). Earthly kings make casual visits to *Indra,* and the list is endless. In no other literate tradition is the concern for man so manifest as to make celestial particiaption in human affairs, on the human level, in human guise, so frequent an occurrence and a matter of norm. Nor is man himself raised to celestial level with such facility elsewhere. In fact, a position even lower than man's may be assigned to gods, for according to *Nāṭyaśāstra*[21] (XXXIV. 18-19) gods are heroes of the second category, *dhīroddhata*, haughty, whereas a commander or a minister of the king is to be depicted as *dhīrodātta*.

Also as *Indra* is king among gods, a king is *Indra* among men. Thus by being equated with celestial beings man is not necessarily placed on an ideal pedestal because the celestial beings are not necessarily even his peers; they are only different and often in need of help from the best of men as much as man also needs them. A liaison or friendship between the two is often established. The celestial, of heaven (*svarga*), and the divine are not identical in Hindu thought. It is the divine that, divided, became man and woman and remains the highest ideal.

LIFE OF INVOLVEMENT

This idealistic interpretation of the *kāvya* can leave many questions unanswered. Is the playwright describing the life as it is or is he setting forth an ideal ? If the latter, does it not, again, leave only a very limited scope for the development of human character ?

The answer to this will support our earlier hypothesis of a *kāvya* view that reconciles the two aspects. The practical, pragmatic life forms the actual subject matter of the *kāvyas*. It would be impossible to develop a drama or any account of human life without a full understanding of man's day-to-day life and situation. If the theoreticians like *Bharata* had not been concerned with man they would not have made and recorded observations on languages, dialects, dress and behaviour patterns in love and life of the peoples of various localities and social strata. Only a careful scrutiny of man could have enabled them to analyze these, set down in specific categories and characterise them. The effort of man, *puruṣārtha* of the religious philosophers, becomes in *kāvya* a fivefold pursuit in stages (*avasthās*) of the plot: (a) *ārambha*, a project is undertaken, (b) *yatna*, active effort is begun as a result of which, (c) *prāptyāśā*, a prospect of success appears, and (d) *niyatāpti*, the main obstacles are removed; finally (e) *phalāgama*, the desired aim is achieved. The emphasis clearly is on action and involvement (*pravṛtti*), not on a denial of life. All emotions are experienced and brought to climax and maturity (*vipāka*). Thus the cosmological religio-philosophic view is presented as it fits the entire scheme of life. Not the tranquil hero, *dhīra-praśānta* but the active and magnanimous *dhīrodātta* is regarded as the ideal man; if the emphasis had been on withdrawal from worldly involvements, *nivṛtti*, the case would have been the reverse.

INDIVIDUAL DISPOSITIONS

In Indian thought a sense of duty and law applicable to each individual (*sva-dharma*) is dictated by his own inner latent potentialities (*vāsanās* and *saṁskāras*), the persons' propensities give them each a specific psychological character. The three main types of personalities are (a) harmonious and full of light (*sāttvika*), the highest; (b) active, restless (*rājasa*), the middling, and (c) inert and full of darkness (*tāmasa*), the lowest. The details of these are well known. The way of life each person follows cannot, thus, be like that of any other and yet it is fully valid as it fits within the framework of the four purposes of man (*caturvarga*) and this reconciliation of the ideal with the practical dictates the view taken in the dramas, biographical poems and the epics. The poet describes a person as and on whatever level he is acting. The description of four types of heroes according to character proves a further recognition of this fact.[22] *Dhīrodātta* is always the highest type, with his magnanimity, steadfastness and depth of character, self-confidence without boastfulness, a harmonious mind. *Rāma* is the prime example of this type. *Dhīroddhata* is haughty, boastful, ambitious, *Dhīralalita* is soft, amorous, luxury-loving and the credit for his success goes to well wishing friends. *Dhīra-praśānta* is sometimes a diluted version of the *dhīra-lalita* but according to *Bhoja* he is the seeker of tranquillity and spiritual peace. *Bhoja* attributes love of virtue (*dharma-śṛṅgāra*) to *dhīrodātta*; love of worldly success (*artha-śṛṅgāra*) to *dhīroddhata*; erotic love (*kāma-śṛṅgāra*) to *dhīra-lalita* and love of spiritual salvation (*mokṣa-śṛṅgāra*) to the *dhīra-praśānta*. Thus each has his own pursuit chosen from *caturvarga* according to his own predisposition and character. What is right behaviour for one type of character would be out of place in another. For example, the question of polygamy. *Vālmīki* and those who have borrowed from him of course nowhere condemn *Daśaratha's* polygamy. They only describe, without a value judgement, what undesirable results and sorrows accrue as a natural result of his polygamy, and go on to extol *Rāma*'s fidelity to one woman. It has not been noticed before that *dhīrodātta* heroes are usually monogamous. *Dhīralalita*, in accordance with their temperament, are described as falling in and out of love, while for the *Dhīroddhata* this pursuit may only be incidental. For *dhīrodātta* fidelity to one woman, the *anukūla* stage, is normal and permanent whereas for *dhīralalita* it is a temporary phase of emotions.

Just as each has his own love from amongst the four purposes of man, so each has his own definition of courage. There are four distinct types of bravery (*vīra-rasa*) *SD*. III. 234: (a) *dharma-vīra*, brave in righteousness, following the path of virtue irrespective of consequences, for example *Yudhiṣṭhira*; (b) *dāna-vīra*, courageous in giving without thought for one's own comfort, for example *Karṇa*; (c) *dayā-vīra*, courageous in compassion, for example *Jīmūtavāhana* giving his own body to *Garuḍa* to feed on in order to save the *Nāgas*; and (d) *yuddha-vīra*, brave in a battle.

A *Kṣatriya* hunts and enjoys pursuing his quarry but as he reaches the boundary of the forest of the hermits, a *tapovana*, he must desist as a brahmin forbids him saying, "your weapon is for protecting the distressed, not to attack the innocent" (*AŚ*. I.2-11).

Not all persons react to strong drink in a uniform way (*Nāṭyaśāstra*, VII. 39-43).[23] The highest, *sāttvika*, type simply falls asleep, the middling laughs and sings aloud whereas the lowest type cries out and curses; some however, have no scope for finding out their reaction as they totally follow the *śāstric* injunction against alcoholic beverages.

The law books recognize a marriage by free love (*gāndharva*) but not as the highest form. There are people who regard themselves wedded to each other without the formalities of a ritual. The dramatist, *Bhāsa* in *Avimāraka*[24] (VI. 14ff.) expresses mute sympathy for the steps taken by the young lovers but at the same time compromises with the *śāstric* view by having the girl *Kuraṅgī's* father say that "I would still prefer a wedding by the sacred fire." "Everyone to his own taste" (*RV*. VI.30).

Nor is the character of a person in *kāvya* fixed permanently. No man is condemned to remain true to a set form of behaviour. A spectator is elevated to the consciousness of a higher type because the actor represents a person who has raised himself to a higher level after passing through many experiences. Evil is only temporary and no villain (*khala-nāyaka* or *pratināyaka*) appears in some of the finest works such as *Śākuntala*, except that the hero himself temporarily appears to be a villain when he is unjust, until he realizes his mistake and repents. There is a change of heart, rather than a vanquishing of an evil person. Even where the villain is shown as incorrigible, other characters temporarily evil are studied with sympathy. *Bhāsa* and *Śūdraka* both in handling *Cārudatta* story have done this in a superb manner. A courteson, *Vasantasenā*, is depicted as a woman loyal to one man in love; she is the *pativratā*, the chaste heroine of the drama. Even though she is endlessly pursued and threatened by some and her house is censord by others (*MK.*[25] IV. 10-17) she proves her fidelity. A thief, *Sajjalaka* in *Bhāsa's* work and *Śarvilaka* in *Śūdraka's*, is forgiven his crime—like a crime of passion, a crime for love even though "a lover is motivated only by self-interest" (*KS.* II.2), that is, he does whatever seems to bring him fulfilment in love, there is rehabilitation from a life of crime when he marries his beloved. In *Bhāsa's* drama he takes monastic vows as a result of the goodness and understanding shown to him. Even though there is no redemption for the arch-villains like *Pālaka* (in *MK.*) and the *Nandas* (in *MR.*), the leading figures like malicious *Śakāra* and the worthy opponent *Rākṣasa* finally change sides. Whatever appears to the playwright to be the divine goodness must finally exert itself, the result of which is all-round happiness; hence no tragedy is allowed.

HUMAN RELATIONS AND SITUATIONS

It is not possible to prepare a summary of all episodes des criptive of each relationship in the *kāvya* and only a few examples may be given. Relationships in all their phases are described even though "everyone thinks himself beautiful" (*AŚ.* II. 7ff.). The ideal must always be maintained as "relationships established by the good people never spoil" (*KS.* VI. 29). Many relationships suggest the memories of a past incarnation (*AM.* II.1) and strong friendships continue from a previous life (*AŚ.* V. 2). A dear person removes one's sorrows without doing anything (*URC.* II.19).

A woman plays many roles. A daughter, she is given away to a husband, as a wife she is loved, or abandoned and exiled, or faces the jealousies of co-wives in palace intrigues. On the other hand rare tributes, sometimes lefthanded, are paid to her.

Duṣyanta who does not recognise *Śakuntalā* says "even non-human females are known to be smart without having been taught, how much more so the women of the intelligent species" (*AŚ.* V.22). According to *MŚ.* (IV. 19) "men become wise by learning texts; women are born naturally learned", and "one can hold a woman only by the heart" (*MŚ.* I 1. 50).

A courtesan may be praised by a man of better culture (*MŚ.* I.57) but often she is either treated as a fair game, by those of low mentality with whom the playwright has no sympathy (*MŚ.* I.17-42; *Cāru.* I.8-25), and censured by those who lack understanding (*MŚ.* IV. 10-17) but she is also acceptable as the wife of a highly honored citizen. "A girl's father has much to worry about" (*AM.* I.2); she is "held only in trust and the father is relieved when she is married off (*AŚ.* IV. 22), yet, "to be a girl's father is to be much honoured as she is sought by so many kings" (*AM.* I.9). A girl's youthful beauty is adored (e. g. *KS.* I.31 ff., *AŚ.* I.20) and a maiden's natural shyness is taken note of (*KS.* VI.84, 91). However, "marriages should be entered into after great consideration" (*AM.* I.2ff.). A man seeks to marry a matching woman, someone who is like himself, *ātmānurūpā* (*RV.* I.33, *KS.* I.18), "a gem uniting with another gem" (*ibid* VI.79) "moonlight to the moon, a Ganges to the ocean" (*ibid.* VI.85), "pleasure (*Rati*) to passion (*Kāma*)" (*ibid.* VII.15) so that "the Lord's creating their forms would have been in vain had they not been thus joined together" (*RV.* VII.14, *KS.* VII.66) and their union is "like adding of rootverb and suffix to each other to form a single word" (XI.56). The descriptions of love between a man and a woman as seen in *kāvya* need no special mention. In *KS.* I., the test of *Pārvatī's* love, in *AŚ.* the falling in love, *URC*'s definition of and tenderness in love both in union and separation are all well known. A woman in love talks to her man as if drinking him (with eyes and ears) (*MŚ.* IV.4ff., *Cāru.* IV.1ff.), and the physical enjoyment of passionate love follows all the rules of sexual science in all *kāvya* works.

Whereas a wife matches a man, a son is his own self and a man is anxious to be born as his own son through his wife

(*RV*. I.33, *KS*. VI.28). One regrets having abandoned a woman in whom he had sown his seed (*AS*. VI.23-25). The child turns out to be a "spark of fire waiting for the fuel in order to blaze" (*ibid*. VII.15). The son is one's own facsimile to whom friends' love should be transferred at one's death (*MŚ*. IX.42). When a child is born, the parents' love for each other only increases rather than be divided (*RV*. III.24). Sanskrit language has a special word for the love one bears for the offs-pring; *vātsalya*. Profuse descriptions of this sentiment may be seen in *RV*. III.4, 17, 25ff., XIV.3ff., *KS*. I.24ff., V.3-5, XI.15ff., *AŚ*. IV.6, 21, VII. 14-19, *MŚ*. X.23, *AM*. VI.3-4, *et al* throughout *kāvya* in the most poetic and touching words.

The pathos of *URC*. in separation of *Rāma* and *Sītā*, *Aja*'s lament at *Indumatī's* death (*RV*. VIII.37ff.) and *Rati*'s cries at *Kāma*'s being burnt to ashes (*KS*. IV.1ff.) are examples of the depth of human feelings among those related. Words of comfort spoken at such occasions (*RV*. VIII. 83ff., XIV. 72ff.) are what a kinsman anywhere may appropriately employ.

Placed in provocative or challenging situations people respond naturally. The assembled kings cannot help but fritter about in anxiety and make gestures expressing of their desire towards *Indumatī* (*RV*. VI.12). As she passes rejecting each one of them, he goes pale with disappointment "like a housefront darkening when left behind by someone carrying a lamp at night" (*RV*. VI.67). Natural excitement of citi-zens rushing to view an important procession (*RV*. VII.6ff.) is recorded in vivid detail. Human selfishness and weaknesses are taken note of; *Duṣyanta* allows the *Vidūṣaka* to leave but for his own secret purpose (*AŚ*. II.2ff.) and a monk is said to be waiting for a secret rendezvous with a labouring woman (*Cāru*. III.9ff.). *Mālavikāgnimitra* relates harem intrigues at their ugliest. The act IX of *MŚ*. records the proceedings of an unjust court of law making decisions under the pressure of the king's malicious brother-in-law, a scene which seems quite from our own times as innocent *Cārudatta* says; "Such judges, who would declare even a crow to be white, disgracing the administration ! Thousands of innocent people have been and continue to be massacred by them" (*MŚ.* IX.41). Even though *MŚ.* is said to be unique in such descriptions, the king's brother-in-law plays the same role in *Kālidāsa's AŚ.* VI (*praveśaka*) and the interrogation of an innocent suspect carried out by the police officers is quite 'modern'. When facing injustice even a timid woman may be provoked to angry exchanges with a king (*AŚ.* V. 21-22) but "a weak man's anger consumes only himself" (*MŚ.* I.55, *Cāru.* I.46). Often one is in a thankless position like that of a king's ministers as "when they are successful (in undertakings of the state) it is the king who gets all the credit, but when they fail the blame falls on them; oh, how subtly a king penalizes a man when he addresses him as his 'minister'" (*AM.* I.5).

The concern for one's reputation is universal. Upon the theft of what had been left as trust, *Cārudatta* resolves to "pay back, even if he has to beg in order to be able to do so" (*MŚ.* III.26).[26] Especially if one had been highly honoured before, the loss of respect can be over-whelming "when friends turn away", "those who have fallen can find no one to seek a favour from", one drinks the "poison of disrepute" (*MŚ.* X. 12-16) alone and says "I am not afraid of dying but I grieve only that my reputation is smeared; if only I were absolved, death to me would be like the birth of a son" (*ibid.* X.27).

The curse of poverty has drawn the special attention of the authors of *MŚ* (I. 8-15, 36-38, 53, III. 19, 24-26, 28, V. 40-43) and *Cāru* (III.14, 15, 17, 18), and "when a woman is so financially independent that she may help a man, their male and female roles are reversed." For other complaints against poverty see *Subhāṣita-ratna-koṣa*[27] verse 3-19 under *dīna-vrajyā* (pp. 230-232) and *Subhāṣita-ratna-bhāṇḍāgara.* 23 verses against the riches (pp. 64 and 65), 15 verses against the rich (p. 65), 87 verses on poverty (pp. 65-68), 48 verses on one who must ask a favour (pp. 73 and 74), 5 verses on the beggar (p. 96), 4 verses on having to be sheltered under another's roof (p. 96), 18 verses on the depressed condition of a servant

(p. 97). These collections alone should suffice to answer the allegations that Sanskrit poets did not pay attention to people's "poverty misery and squalor".[29] Quite rightly, therefore, Professor Daniel H.H. Ingalls expresses disagreement with Kosambi and Gokhale's[30] derogatory view of the poems in *Vidyākara*'s anthology.

The beating heart of a thief (*MŚ.* III.10) and the plight of an escaped prisoner (*ibid.* VI.12ff.) all such situations of man have drawn the writers' sympathy. *AM.* (IV. 1-5) has the most impressive description of a man wandering alone and thirsty under a hot sun looking for his beloved and finally attempting suicide. Less unhappy are people's boasts; confidence of a thief in his mastery of the art (*MŚ.* III.21, *Cāru.* III.11), false boasts that only make the listeners suspicious (*Cāru.* I.13), laughable, foolish statements like, "I can kill a hundred women; after all I am a brave man" (*MŚ.* I. 28ff.). An example of sarcasm may be seen in the interrogation of a suspect by the police officers (*AŚ.* VI. *praveśaka*) :

Guards (beating) :	You, *Kumbhīraka*, where did you find this jewelled ring embossed with the king's name ?
Man (showing fear) :	Please, gentlemen; I am not a man of that type.
One Guard :	So then, the king himself gave it to you as a gift because you are such a good looking brahmin, eh ?
Man :	Listen, I am a fisherman living at the village of *Śakrāvatāra*.
Other Guard	Idiot! Did we ask you your caste ?

Or take a quotation given by *Rudraṭa* (*Kāvyālaṅkāra*[31] VII.20), "he is emasculate, ugly, foolish, malicious, and hurts (others) on (their) tender spots; yet strange, he is not a rich man !" Numerous examples of this type can be given. We have intentionally left out the retorts of *vidūṣakas* as they have been studied in detail by two authors.[32]

The human psychology and conflicts of conscience and consciousness are dealt with expertly. In excitement, speech becomes confused, e.g. "making a thief in the wall a hole has come in" (*Cāru.* III. 14ff). A guilty man looks pale and thinks that everyone is looking at him (IV.1, 6) One interprets another's speech according to his own state of mind (*Veṇīsaṁhāra* II.49ff.; *Mudrārākṣasa* I.6) and the playwright succeeds in conveying this by a play on words. Dreams as expressive of impressions and desires of the subconscious are well known from the time of *Bhāsa*, (*Svapnavāsovadattam* V.8ff.). Sometimes one wonders whether one is not dreaming (*SV.* VI. 17), whether "this is a dream, a magical trick, a confusion of mind" (*AŚ.* VI.10), one has dreamlike visions while awake (*Cāru.* IV.7ff.). Memories transport a person to quite another place and time (*URC.* I. 17ff.). Sometimes confusion so prevails that one's intelligence becomes "like a reflection in the mirror, left side appearing on the right and the right side appearing on the left" (*MŚ.* I. 16ff.). It becomes difficult to make a choice: upon recognising *Śiva*, *Pārvatī* could "neither stand still nor walk forward" (*KS.* V. 85), and *Duṣyanta* can "neither accept (*Śakuntalā*) to enjoy her nor can he altogether reject her" (*AŚ.* V. 19). One is so torn between duty and love that to the public *Rāma* declares, "Giving up love, pity, comforts and even (beloved) *Sītā* for the sake of the people I have no hesitation" (*URC.* I. 12) but when alone, "hearing his cries (for *Sītā*) even a stone could cry, even the heart of *vajra* would burst" (*URC.* I. 28). *Duṣyanta* is facing a dilemma: "On one hand the ascetics' need, on the other an elder's command. Neither can be transgressed. Which must I do ?" The *Vidūṣaka* has the easy answer: "Well, be a *Triśaṅku* and hang in the middle !" (*AŚ.* 2, 16ff.). The chain of causation seems to fail. The figures *vibhāvanā*, *viśeṣokti*, *asaṅgati*, and *viṣama* (*SD.* X.66, 67, 69, 70) deal with this and the figure of *virodha* is employed where genus, attribute, act and substance do not correspond to their own nature or mutual natural connection (*SD.* X. 67, 68). "The heart is bursting but doesn't split into two, the personality is in a state of swoon without entirely losing consciousness, an inner fire burns the body but does not quite turn it to ashes, cruel fate hits at the tender sports but does not completely kill."

(*URC.* III. 33).

Schizophrenic situations arise and one curses himself while unable to draw away from a course of action: *Rāma* gets ready to kill the outcaste ascetic *Śambūka* but not without an outburst; "Wield this dagger, my right hand ! Have you not already shown your expertise in pushing *Sītā* into exile ? Wherefore can you have any compassion left ?" But, once again, as tragedy is not allowed, the crisis is overcome through conciliation. *Śambūka* ascends to *Rāma's* own celestial world. *Duṣyanta* regrets an earlier hasty step, "When my beloved herself had come to me I abandoned her; now I live by her portrait alone. I crossed the stream of abundant flowing water and now I seek to quench my thirst on a mirage" (*AŚ.* VI.16).

He repents and confesses frankly that "some confusion of the mind had overcome me then and I must have been for the moment a blind man pushing away a garland from his neck thinking it a snake" (*ibid.* VII.24). There is always a a change of attitude, a reconciling of mental conflict, a conversion to harmony.

MAN AND NATURE

The *kāvya* view of nature can be seen on two levels. 1) Man appreciates nature. In works of poetry this is natural and Sanskrit *kāvya* is no exception. *Ṛtusaṁhāra*, *Meghadūta*, *RV.* IX. 25ff; XVI.43; *KS.* I. 1-16; III.24ff; VIII. 53ff; *AŚ.* I.3, 4; IV.2; *SV.* I. 16; *AM.* II.12; *IV.*11 *et al*, on various beauties of nature; *RV.* V. 6; XIV. 78; *KS.* V. 14 on trees and many such examples are well known to the erudite.[33] Love of animals is seen in *RV.* V. 7; *KS.* V. 35; *AŚ.* I. 7, 10, 14, 15; II. 6, and even though hunting is a royal hobby (*RV.* IX. 55-67; *AŚ.* I. 6-9; II. 5), the beauty of some animals reminds the hunter of his beloved so he lets them alone (*RV.* IX. 48, 67; *AŚ.* II.3) or is forbidden to hunt by peaceful hermits (*AŚ.* I. 10, 11). (2) Man and nature interact as there is a chord of sympathy between them. (a) Sometimes this is only a poetic device. As *Daśaratha* rules over *Ayodhyā* the forces of nature, seasons, flower shrubs, all attend upon him to serve him and to make life pleasant for his subjects (*RV*. ·X. 24ff.). (b) Man enters into kinship relation with nature so that *Śakuntalā* treats the trees and vines of her father's hermitage as persons. It is not a mere poetic simile as in (*AŚ*. IV. 13) but a personal experience as in the heroine's dialogue with her friends while watering the plants (*ibid.* I. 17ff.). (c) There is a religious personification and deification of the forces of nature following the general Hindu tradition. Two random examples: *Sītā*, flanked by personified Ganges and mother earth, rising up from the water (*URC*. VII. 1), and the *Viṭa*'s argument against committing murder at a lonely spot; "the ten quarters, forest deities, moon, this sun with brilliant rays, *dharma*, the winds, the sky, my own inner self and this earth as a witness of all rights and wrongs—these are watching me" (*MŚ*. VIII. 24). (d) Nature is represented as truly responding to man's moods and situations. Pregnant *Sītā*'s grief is shared by all birds and beasts as she is abandoned in the forest; "(as)...she began to weep, peacocks stopped their dances, trees (dropped) their blossoms, does no longer grazed" (*RV*. XIV. 68, 69). *Śakuntalā's* departure so saddens nature that "creepers seem to shed tears" and "a deer who was like an adopted son, brought up by her on little handfuls of grain, is blocking her way" (*AŚ*. IV. 12, 14). Since by the king's command there would be no celebration of spring festivities, "though the sprouts appeared long ago, the mango tree does not blossom, the *kurabaka* blossom does not flower, and the *kokila* bird's coo is thwarted in its throat..." (*AŚ*. VI. 4). At *Raghu*'s birth "all quarters became pleasant and calm (*praseduḥ*), breezes blew soft, the flames of the sacred ritual fire turned towards the right (as a good omen) and everything indicated auspiciousness; the birth of such (personages) is indeed for the elevation of the world (around)" (*RV*. III.14). The last line hints at the view taken elsewhere that (e) man may indeed influence nature by his will so that nature miraculously provides him with his need (*AŚ*. V. 9). Man's evil may also adversely affect the nature so as to stunt its growth;

"Have the trees of the *Aśrama* forests) stopped growing because of my sins ?"—asks King *Duṣyanta* (AŚ V. 9). It is, therefore, necessary for man to keep up certain ideals otherwise his entire natural environment would become unpleasant.

HUMAN IDEALS

In *kāvya*, man is seen pursuing ideals with all his strength. *Aja* accepts rulership as an act of obedience to his father and not for any enjoyment of (power or) pleasures (*RV.* VIII.2). *Śiva*'s marriage is not for a selfish reason but to do a requested favour to the gods (*KS.* VI. 26ff.). *Rāma* maintains his poise and equilibrium "whether wearing silks in preparation for a coronation or putting on bark clothing when ordered into exile" (*RV.* XII.8). Whether the ideals are universal or only results of peculiar social conventions, the characters find strength to pursue them. *Dhāraṇī* is at first jealous but later bedecks *Mālavikā*, the prince's new choice of a bride, because "good loving women serve their husbands even through the rivals; great rivers take along other streams to the ocean " (*MA.* V. 19), and *Śakuntalā* is advised to "treat the co-wives like dear friends" (*AŚ.* IV.18). These may appear to be extreme examples and it may be argued that here *Dhāraṇī* and *Śakuntalā* obviously have no other choice, but men with complete freedom of action also choose the path of duty and ideal in spite of great discomfort to themselves. *Yaugandharāyaṇa*, the minister, in *Svapnavāsavadattam* and *Pratijñāyaugandharāyaṇa* is a prime example of self-sacrifice. In *RV.* I. 76, king *Dilīpa* is racing to meet his wife after a long absence, not out of physical desire but because he must not transgress the religious rule that a householder must sexually unite with his wife at least once a month after her menstruation. *Cāṇakya* holds all power over the king who is his disciple and would gladly provide any luxuries but like a good brahmin the minister must continue to lead the life of an ascetic hermit living in a broken down thatched hut devoting himself to teaching his disciples (*MR.* II.15).

Śiva must interrupt his love-play for the evening prayers

(*KS.* VIII. 47ff.) and a policeman states categorically that while on duty "I do not know my own father" (*MŚ.* VI.15). From a god to a policeman, passing through all psychological weaknesses and crises of conscience as seen earlier, man of every status and on every level must choose the right.

IDEAL PERSONALITY

Neither sex (*KS.* VI.2, *URC.* IV. 11) nor age (*URC.* IV. 11 *RV.* XI.1) are a barrier to attaining a high and exalted personality, respected by all. Just as a noble man's presence may evoke nature's beauty and harmony, so a good spirit abides in a beautiful body. The allegedly negative attitudes of Indian thought towards the body are not found in the *kāvya* which delights in beauty. "Body is the prime means of virtue" (*KS.* V. 34) and "features cannot but bespeak the character" (*MŚ.* XI.16). The *kāvya* works, therefore, go to some lengths in describing a hero's physical appearance (*RV.* III.34, *et al*).

We have spoken above of the four types of hero of whom *udātta*, the magnanimous, is the highest. While to understand others is to understand the reality as it exists, to understand him is to pursue an ideal state, in an ideal city. As *udātta's* first love is of virtue, *dharma*, to understand *dharma* is to understand him. The most comprehensive description of this nature of the ideal man is found in *Śṛṅgāra-prakāśa* of *Bhoja* (*Ch.* XVIII. pp. 36, 37)[34] as follows

> "*Dharma* is the conduct as prescribed in the revealed and legal texts (*śruti* and *smṛti*). It is of three kinds: acting, refraining, and (following) rules. Action is of ten kinds, 'being done by' speech, mind and body. '(4 plus 3 plus 3 = 10).'
>
> Speech beneficial (to others), pleasant, truthful and noble.
>
> Mind: Having faith (in God and life after), compassionate, and not greedy after others' possessions.

> Body: Serving the preceptor (*guru*), charity, protection offered to the distressed. Refraining from ten activities, of which 'five are missing in the MS.', the other five being: cruelty, desire for others' wealth, use of forbidden things, theft and violence.
>
> The rules of self-control are also tenfold, concerning speech, mind and body; accepting causation (so the sacred rituals lead one to heaven), loyalty to one's own caste rules, relationship with the kindred, avoiding the company of those who are opposed both to the popular and textual norms, earning livelihood equitably, not transgressing the elders' command, not refusing a request, keeping one's promise, not turning away in a battle, laying down one's life for (the protection of) cows and brahmins etc."

The qualities of an *udātta* hero make a formidable and inspiring list

> "absence of pride at success, no depression at bereavement and such, no dejection in adversities, no break in *dharma* rules through other attractions, competing with the best against fearsome surprises, aversion to lowly tendencies, forgiveness in spite of power, repentence over negligent slips, respect towards noble conduct, frank acceptance of others' good qualities, not rejoicing at others' adversities, no interest in ill speaking about others, anger only at the deserving, carrying on an undertaking to the last, no amazement at one's own multitude of feats, no pride of caste and such.."

The list continues and *Bhoja* quotes from *kāvya* works to present an example for each. The quality of *dhairya* which characterises *dhīrodātta* is defined as "the habit of the mind not to allow senses to be affected", so that pride, intolerance, malice, jealousy and so forth do not arise in a man "even when causes for these are present" (*ibid.* p. 37).

The total effect of the presence of such a personality on

any scene can be presented by describing a perfect state as we shall now see. The final benediction, *bharota-vākya*, in a *kāvya* matches in sentiments the ideas expressed at the end of (a) the Hindu rituals, and (b) an epic like the *Rāmāyaṇa*. The examples follow :

Bharata-vākya :

(1) "May the cows be rich with milk and the earth be prosperous with all grains;
May the clouds rain in time and the breezes blow soothing to the minds of all men;
May all who are born be joyous and the good brahmins[35] be venerated;
May the glorious kings, firm in virtue and with enemies pacified, guard the earth" (*MŚ*. X. 61)

(2) May all get across the difficulties
May all come by happy events;
May all realize their wishes;
May all be joyous everywhere (or, in all matters).
(*VU*[36] V. 25)

(3) May cows and brahmins always be taken care of;
May comfort (and happiness) accrue to all citizens.
(*AM*. VI. 21[37])

Ritual Prayers

(1) May all men be happy (and in comfort[38]);
May all things be auspicious;
May there be continuous growth. (*Nityāhnikam*[39] p. 66)

(2) (i) May the wicked become good men, and may the good attain peace;
May those at peace be freed from bondage and may the free release others.
(ii) Well it be with the people;

May rulers safeguard the earth, taking the path of justice and righteousness;
May it ever be well with the cows and the brahmins;
May all people be happy and in comfort.[38]

(iii) May the clouds rain at the (right) time and the earth be rich with grain;
May this country be free of anguish and may the brahmins be free of fear.

(iv) May all be in comfort and all be free of disease;
May all come by happy events and may sorrow be no man's share. (*Prayers, Praises, Psalms* pp. 323 and 324)

The Epic, Rāmāyaṇa[40]

The brother of *Lakṣmaṇa*, the splendrous *Rāma*, whose arms reached up to the knees and who had a wide chest, ruled over the earth. 96.
Then no widows lamented, and there was no danger from preying beasts nor from diseases while *Rāma* administered the kingdom. 98.
The localities were free of prowlers and no one suffered anything untoward, elders then did not have to perform younger ones' last rites. 99.
All around was happiness and all were intent on virtue; looking at *Rāma* they refrained from being violent to each other. 100.
They lived a hundred years and had many sons; (they were) free of sicknesses and without sorrows as *Rāma* managed the kingdom. 101.
The trees were ever-flowering, ever fruitful and wide in the trunks; the clouds rained at (right) time and the breeze was pleasant to the touch. 102. (*Yuddha-kāṇḍa sarga* 128)

It is obvious that the ideal state of man prayed for in the rituals, aspired for through the themes and plots dealing with heroes and characters of various levels and types is finally realized in the *udātta*, the highest type of hero who is physically and morally perfect and therefore, by his mere presence, capable of bringing benevolent changes in the society and in nature around him. What is an aspiration expressed by the optative, imperative and benedictive in the *bharata-vākyas* is a reality of the ideal state in the epic, so that the latter embodies both the description of what ought to be and what is—the two then are one. The epic thus becomes both a work of poetry and a text on law. The description of the ideal state, however, is not limited to the epic and is found in other *kāvyas* wherever an *udātta* hero leads, as we have seen above.

To conclude : (1) The *kāvya* works need to be studied in detail, as to philosophy of life and conceptions about man implied in their themes and plots or expressed in words. (2) (a) Such a study will support our view that the *kāvya* attitude to man is not pessimistic, does not propose withdrawal from worldly realities but rather that it is pragmatic, concerned with the individual, indicating a life of involvement with daily problems, experiences and emotions (b) and finally through the agency of an ideal hero, *dhīrodātta*, it aims at the universals being employed to serve the particulars and thereby bringing a perfect state to the individual citizen (*nagara*, *jana*, *prajā*, *lokāḥ*) as well as to the society (*grāma*, *pura*, *janapada*, *deśa*) and the environment as a whole.

APPENDIX

Raghuvaṁśa X. 15-32 (to *Viṣṇu*)

15. The gods fell at his feet and addressed their praises to him who is the pacifier of their enemies, the one to whom praise are due and who is beyond the grasp of speech or mind.

16. Salutations to you who first creates, then bears and then withdraws the world, you whose self abides thus threefold.

17. Just as the rain water, naturally sweet, takes on other tastes when falling at various places, so also you, by nature immutable, take up various conditions in (conjunction with) the *guṇas*.

18. Immeasurable you measure the worlds, seeking nothing you grant what is sought. Unconquered you are victorious, and entirely unmanifest you are the cause of the manifest.

19. They (the wise) know you as living in the heart yet distant, free of desires yet practising asceticism, compassionate yet untouched by sin, ancient yet free of decay.

20. Omniscient you are unknown, origin of all you are self-existent; Lord of all you are masterless, though one you divide into all forms.

21. They say that you are sung of in the seven *sāmans*, you rest in the waters of seven oceans, you have in your mouth the seven fires and you are the sole support of seven worlds.

22. From you who have four faces (arises) knowledge with its fourfold fruit (*dharma*, *artha*, *kāma*, *mokṣa*) and the four states of time (the four *yugas*), as well as the people with their fourfold divisions of *varṇas*.

23. For emancipation the *yogins* with mind controlled by practice concentrate on you who are as light living in (their) hearts.

24. Who knows the true reality of you ? You take birth though unborn, you destroy the enemies though without movement, you are asleep yet ever wakeful.

25. Yours is the power to enjoy the objects such as sound, to observe the most difficult ascetic practices, to guard (your) progeny—and yet remain a (neutral) witness.

26. Many paths, the ways to attainment, diversified by various teachings, all lead to you as *Gaṅgā's* floodwaters into the ocean.

27. For proper withdrawal (i.e. cessation of *saṁsāra*) you alone are the resort of those dispassionate ones whose minds have entered into you and who have surrendered their actions to you.

28. Though you may be known by direct perception, your glory is not limited to (the forms of) this earth and such; how can one state whether you are to be proved by inference or by the prophets' word of revelation ?

29. Since you purify men by mere remembrance, the fruits of all acts (and tendencies) are offerings unto you.

30. Like gems in the ocean, like splendours of the sun, your acts are beyond the power of any hymnal praise.

31. Nothing is unattained, yet to be attained, of you. Only kindness towards the world is the reason for your taking birth and performing actions.

32. Singing your glory if speech is silenced it is through our weariness and incapacity and not because this is the limit of your attributes.

Kumpārasambhavo II. 3-15

3. Then they (the gods) fell before him, the sustainer of all, the Lord of speech with faces in all directions, and stood addressing him with meaningful words.

4. Salutations to you of three forms, the absolute one self before creation, who then became divided, apportioning the three *guṇas*.

5. As you sowed the unfailing seed in the waters and from that arose the moving and unmoving (things of) the world, you are glorified as its source, O Unborn One.

6. Though one, you emanate your power through three conditions, having become the cause of dissolution, continuity and creation.

7. Man and woman are your two halves as you split your form with intent to create; they are then the birth-givers of the creation and are called its parents.

8. The sleeping and waking of you, whose nights and days are divided by the measure of your own time, is the dissolution and creation of things.

9. Without origin, you are the origin of the world; endless, the end of the world. Beginningless, you are the beginning of the world; without a master, the Lord of the world.

10. You know self by self, you create self by self; with self having done the work you dissolve back into the very self.

11. Liquid or compressed solid, gross or subtle, light or heavy, manifest or otherwise—you make yourself as you wish.

12. You are the origin of (*Vedic*) speech which begins with *Om*, is chanted with three pitch tones, has sacrifice as its application and heaven as its fruit.

13. (The wise) consider you as Nature (*prakṛti*) which functions for the sake of Person (*puruṣa*); the very you they also know as the Person, the neutral witness of *prakṛti*.

14. You are Father even of forefathers, Deity of the deities, farther even than beyond and ordainer even of ordainers.

15. You alone are the oblation as well as the priest, the enjoyable and the eternal enjoyer; knowable and the knower, the meditating one as well as the supreme object of meditation.

VI. 75-77

75. (He is *Śiva*—) endowed with the powers such as to become minute, who, together with the crescent, bears high the name 'Lord' (*Iśvara*) not applicable to any other,—

76. who upholds this world with his (eight) selves such as the earth, complementing each other's capacity as horses (hold) a chariot on the path,—

77. on whom, functioning within the field, the *yogins* concentrate and whose place, the wise say, is free of the danger of return (to the cycle of *saṁsāra*).

Some of the opening passages (*nāndī*) of the dramas are equally important.

Abhijñāna-śākuntala I. 1

That which was the creator's first creation, that which bears the properly offered oblations, the priestly one, the two that set the time, the one whose attribute is sound and pervades the entire universe, that which is termed nature (*prakṛti*) of all beings, and that by which all animate beings have life-breath—with all these directly perceivable eight aspects of his, may the Lord (*Śiva*) protect you all.

Vikramorvaśīya I. 1.

He, whom they call in the *Vedānta* One Person pervading both worlds; whose exact title of Lord (*īśvara*) applies to no other; whom seekers of deliverance search for within, their vital breaths and such well-controlled; who is easily gained through yoga of devotion; may He, the absolute Lord, lead you to the highest good.

Though the realism of *Śūdraka's Mṛcchakaṭika* is well known, his *nāndī* (I.1) is worthy of attention :

> Knees folded and feet knotted with a double coil of his snake, his senses suspended as all perceptions have ceased through withholding of the vital breath within and processes withdrawn as he, with his vision of truth, sees the (identity of) self within self,—may *Śiva's samādhi* of total absorption in *Brahman* caused by the view of *Śūnya* protect you.

Such verses also serve to show the traditional Indian syncretism and a non-sectarian outlook in which homage is paid to Transcendental *Brahman, Puruṣa,* as well as personalized manifestations—*Prajāpati, Viṣṇu, Śiva,* all equally, and Buddhist *śūnya* is also given a place. *Kālidāsa* is articulate on this attitude, *vide Raghuvaṁśa* X.26. Some of the earliest hymns (*stotras*) to Puranic deities are to be found in works of *Kālidāsa*; of these are quoted above *R.V.* X. 16-32 to *Viṣṇu, KS.* II. 4-15 to *Prajāpati,* VI. 75-77 to *Śiva, AŚ.* I. 1 and *VU.* I. 1 also to *Śiva*; in addition, *KS.* VI. 66-73 to *Himālaya,* X. 17-23 to *Agni,* X. 29-36 to *Gaṅgā,* and *R.V.* I.1 to *Siva* and *Pārvatī*.

While *Kālidāsa's* philosophy is universal, *Bhavabhūti* is more pronounced in his sympathy for the Vedantic doctrine of *vivarta* in which the manifestations of external reality are mere whirls in a sheet of water. He does not have the cause to state it in detail in his dramas but alludes to it in similes and metaphors. His own *opus* is but Word-God, (*śabda-brahman*) transmuted, come to *pariṇāma* (*URC.* VII.20). *Vālmīki* is said to have brought out a modulation, *vivarta* of divine Speech (VI.20) Not the external conditions (*upādhis*) but something else that is innermost in man is the vessel of true love (VI. 12). The pathetic sentiment alone is manifested in the form of various other *rasas* which are merely *vivartas,* like bubbles rising in water (III.47). The word *advaita* (non-duality) is used in a slightly different sense to define love (I. 39) and an agitation (*vikāra*) of senses confuses the consciousness (I. 35).

NOTES

1. Hajime Nakamura, *Ways of thinking of Eastern Peoples*, (East-West center press, Honolulu, 1964). Ch. 2.

2. S. Radhakrishnan and P. T. Raju, *The Concept of Man* (George Allen and Unwin Ltd., London, 1966). pp. 222-223, 233ff.

3. For example, (i) *Bhagavadgītā*, XV.18; (ii) *Patañjali's Mahābhāṣya* (Motilal Banarsidass, Delhi, 1967) *āhnika* I, pp. 6, 40, *et al.*

4. *Mahābhāṣya, āhnika I, vārtikas* ii-iii, pp. 50ff. "Śāstra rules on the propriety of what might otherwise be common vulgar usage of words." *Patañjali* elaborates on the topic by giving examples from problems of dietary laws, fasts in preparation to the ceremony of sacred thread and rules in other ritual observances.

5. Ramarajan Mukherji, *Literary Criticism in Ancient India*, (Sanskrit Pustak Bhandar, Calcutta, 196), pp. 8ff.

6. *Bhoja's Śṛṅgāra-prakāśa*, summary by Dr. V. Raghavan (Madras, 1963), pp. 36-37.

7. *Abhinavagupta's Dhvanyāloka-locanam*, ed., Jagannath Pathak, (Chowkhamba, Varanasi, 1965), p. 41.

8. V. Raghavan, *The Number of Rasas*, Adyar, 1940.

9. (i) *Rudraṭa's Kāvyālaṅkāra*, ed., Satyadev Chaudhari, (Vasudeva Prakasana, Delhi), 1965. XV. 17-19. (ii) For further details see Satyadeva Choudhary, *Essays on Indian Poetics* (Vasudeva Prakashana, Delhi, 1965), pp. 4.78-8

10. In presenting such a view *Kāvya* is not a section unique in Indian literature but follows the general pattern of Indian mind which is also not exclusive. There is no doubt that the treatment of the universe as a composite whole, to view man in relation with the macrocosmos, comprising *dharma*, is one of the first essentials of the Indian mind. This is not limited to texts on religion and philosophy but treatises on any science devote their beginning chapters to discussing this theme and pointing out that the science being taught is to be viewed in the totality of the knowledge of the universe. *Manu's* lawbook starts with a question on *dharma*, answering it with the conceptions about cosmology and creation, goes on to lay down man's duties in social, political, economic, family and all the other facets of life and rounds off at the end describing the results of man's action to the degree of its accord with the law and a rejoinder for striving after the final deliverance, *mokṣa*. *Caraka-saṃhitā*, (ed , Taradatta Pant, Haridas Sanskrit Series, Varanasi, 1937), one of the earliest works on medical science, devotes several chapters to the very theme, analyzing man's mind and activity of his senses in the cosmic experience, advising a virtuous life (*Sūtrasthāna* I.15, 39-58; VII.54-62; VIII; X-XIII.3; XX.3; XXI.34-38; XXV-XXVI.34; XXX.1-25; *Vimānasthāna* I.16-43; VIII.I-126; Śārirasthāna I; II; III.) states the purpose of medical study to be "beneficial to man both for this and the next world" (I.43) by lengthening his life span to provide him time for the practice of *dharma*-(I.16) and an opportunity to serve others with his knowledge of the science

(I.27). *Caraka* details the ethical conduct of man, and renunciation of three desires, *eṣaṇas*; even a discussion on valid proofs of knowledge is included. Suśruta follows the same scheme. Compare this with *Kumārasambhava* V 34; "body indeed is the first means for practising *dharma.*" A work so secular and apparently machiavellian as *Kauṭalya's Arthaśāstra* devotes its first chapter to prove that "a candle to illuminate all sciences, the sole means of all actions, and ever the container of all *dharmas* is the science of metaphysics, *ānvīkṣikī*" (I.i.2) and at the end of the 2nd chapter goes on to state that "therefore, the king must allow no transgression of people's *dharma*, for only by strengthening *dharma* of each he rejoices in this world and in the next. The world is made happy and saved from a sad end only when the noble code is well ordered, *varṇas* and *āśramas* well established and all are guarded with the triple (revealed) texts." (I. ii. 3-4).
It would be illogical to state that these texts place undue emphasis on other-worldly pursuits and ignore man in this world. They succeed only in presenting a balanced view. Otherwise no texts on material sciences and law could have been written. Looking at the scheme followed in the organization of these texts one concludes that the bulk of the texts deals with artha and *kāma* but sandwiches these between *dharma* and *mokṣa*.

11. *Abhijñānaśākuntala*. To cite *Kālidāsa* we have used *kālidāsa-granthāvali*, ed.., Rama Pratapa Tripathi (Kitab Mahal, Ilahabad, 1965).

12. *Bhavabhūti's Uttararāmacarita*, ed. P. V. Kane and C. N. Joshi (Motilal Banarsidass, Delhi, 1962).

13. Prose passages in dramas are being cited by giving the number of a preceding *śloka*.

14. *Raghuvaṁśa*.

15. *Kumārasambhava*.

16. For greater details see S. N. Shastri, *The Laws and Practice of Sanskrit Dramas*, (Chowkhamba, Varanasi), 1961, pp. 3-15.

17. *Ibid.* pp. 19, 23.

18. The Hindu thought is peculiar in that distinctions between human and the divine are vague. The *aṁśāvatāra* theory appears on several levels as follows. (1) All individual souls, *jīvas*, are part emanations from God and thus carry His divine nature. "My own eternal part having become a soul in the world of the living controls the mind and the five senses which abide in their nature"—BhG. XV. 7. (2) Many of the incarnations are *aṁśāvatāras*. "Whenever there is decline of virtue and rise of evil I create *a part of* myself (*ātmāṁśam*) forth—" *BhG.* (Kashmir text) IV. 7. "Whatever essence is endowed with any special power, glory or strength, that you should know to have sprung from a part of my splendour"—*BhG.* X.41. It is with this background that in India a person of high accomplishments is given the epithet 'sprung from a fragment of the divine', *divyāṁśa-samudbhava*, even though it may be only a minute aspect of Godly nature that has descended in him. (3) The part emanation, or even a complete incarnation is not always easily distinguishable from other persons. See *Mahābhārata*, *Aśvamedhaparvan* (Poona edition, 1960).

"Transmigrating, I appear among many species (or, races) for the protection of virtue and to establish virtue."

"When I appear in the *deva* race I conduct everything like a *deva*; (there is) no doubt (about it)."

"When I appear in the *gandharva* race I conduct everything like a *gandharva*; (there is) no doubt (about it)", and......

Similarly "among the *nāgas*, *yakṣas*, and *rākṣasas*"......

"While in my human form they (the *kauravas*) were pitifully requested by me (to desist) but they (were so) deluded that they did not take my advice." 53.16-19.

20. *Viśvanātha's Sāhityadarpaṇa*, ed., Satyavrat Singh, (Chowkhamba, Varanasi), 1963).

21. *Rāmacandra* and *Guṇacandra's Nāṭyadarpaṇa*, ed., G. K. Shrigondekar, (Gaekwad Oriental Series XLVIII, Baroda, 1929), I. 5, p. 27

Bharata's Nāṭyaśāstra, Vol. II., ed., Manomohan Ghosh. (Asiatic Society, Calcutta, 1956).

22. S. N. Shastri, *op. cit.* pp. 204ff.

23. *Bharata's Nāṭyaśāstra*, vol. I., ed., Manomohan Ghosh, (Manisha Granthalaya, Calcutta, 1967).

24. For all *Bhāsa's* works we have used *Bhāsa-nāṭaka-cakram*, ed., Anantaram Shastri, (Chowkhamba, Varanasi, 1963).

25. *Śūdraka's Mṛcchakaṭika*, ed., M. R. Kale, (Booksellers Publishing Co., Bombay, 2nd ed., 1962).

26. Somewhat similar is the theme of Guy de Maupassant's story, *The Necklace*.

27. *Vidyākara's Subhāṣitaratnakoṣa*, ed., D. D. Kosambi and V. V. Gokhale, (Harvard Oriental Series 42, 1957).

28. *Subhāṣita-ratna-bhāṇḍāgāram*, ed., Narayan Ram Acharya, (Nirnaya Sagar Press, Bombay, 8th ed., 1952).

29. Dev Raj Chanana, *The Sanskritist and Indian Society*, in *Inquiry* Monsoon 1965, pp. 49-67. All the arguments presented by Chanana can be refuted by looking through the eleven thousand verses of *Subhāṣita-ratna-bhāṇḍāgāram*

30. *Op. cit.* pp. 50-53

31. *Namisādhu's Tippaṇa* on *Rudraṭa's Kāvyālaṅkāra*, edition cited above, VII. 20 (p. 204).

32. (i) G. K. Bhat, *The Vidūṣaka*, (The New Order Book Co., Ahmedabad, 1959). (ii) J.T. Parikh, *Sanskrit Comic Characters*, (The Popular Book Store, Surat, 1962).

Both these authors have failed to notice that the *vidūṣaka's* primary position is that of a confidante, a close friend, a pal. It is obvious in *Svapnavāsavadatta* Act IV, and *MŚ*. X. where *Cārudatta* who is condemned to death leaves his son in the trusted *vidūṣaka's* care and in *AM*. (IV. 21) the hero is quite lucid; "It would be better if he (the *vidūṣaka*) hears of my escape otherwise the (poor) brahmin will surely collapse. What are any of my enterprises without him ? Source of laughs in gatherings, a fighter in battles, spiritual advisor at (moments of) grief, courageous before (my) enemies, a great festival for my heart—why say too much, he is just my own other body." He is not a clown because his mirth is commandeered by a despot but because out of affection he wants to keep his heavily burdened royal friend laughing, to lessen the weight of office.

33. See Nirmala Upadhyaya, *Kālidāsa kā Prakṛti Citraṇa*, (Nilabha Prakashana, Ilahabad, 1968).

34. We have incorporated Dr. Raghavan's phrases, inside single quotation marks in our translation here as he left much of the text untranslated.

35. This type of the Indian concern for educator, philosopher and priest may be interpreted in many ways and need not be discussed here.

36. Cp. Dr. V. Raghavan, *Prayers, Praises and Psalms*, (G.A. Natesan and Co., Madras, 2nd ed., 1938) p. 324.

37. This is one verse before the *Bharata-vākya* (VI.22).

38. *Sukhin* has to be translated in two words as *sukha* incorporates both happiness as a state of mind as well as the physical comfort and enjoyment.

39. *Nityāhnikam*, ed., Anantarama Śāstrin, (R. S. Vadhyar & Sons, Palghat, 1962).

40. *Vālmīki's Rāmāyaṇa*, ed., Śivarāma Śarmā Vāsiṣṭha, (Chowkhamba, Varanasi, 1957).